Bob—

Thanks for all your
encouragement last year.
I hope you like my
first book.

All Best—
Joan

WHAT WE ALL WISH POLITICIANS UNDERSTOOD

Jason A. Atkinson

LOYAL

What We All Wish Politicians Understood
Published by Loyal Publishing, Inc.

Copyright 2006 Jason A. Atkinson

International Standard Book Number: 1-929125-45-3
Loyal Publishing, Inc.
P O Box 1414, Bend, Oregon 97709

DEDICATION

To my Dad, who taught me
to swim upstream and to Stephanie who thought
I could, would, and who still wanted to.

*I must agree with the farmer I met
on the campaign trail last fall who told me,
"Jason, you're ok, but I think
your wife is beautiful".*

Contents

THE LAST DOORBELL

'm not going to lose this election by just one vote.
That's what I told myself, turning around and
walking back to the last farmhouse. Hot, sweaty,
and tired from six hours of non-stop door-to-door campaigning, that house seemed a mile away. Walking all day
under a bright sun, asking people to elect me as their state
representative, I was tired of hearing my own voice. The
crisply pressed shirt I had started the day with was now
wrinkled and wet with sweat. My "clean cut" look was left
somewhere on the sidewalk about fifty homes back.

The white gate swung unevenly on one hinge. The
second step up the front porch bent under my weight and
the screen door creaked as it was pulled back. I twisted
the old-fashioned door ringer in the center of the door,
and waited in candidate autopilot.

The door flew open, and there she was: frazzled, tired,
a single mom who'd just gotten off work, makeup slightly

running from the heat. She was trying to get her household of three kids (who each had a friend over) under control.

I felt like that guy who always calls at dinner time wanting to sell you something. I was the last thing she needed or wanted to see on her doorstep right then.

"Yes. Can I help you?" she said with forced politeness, pulling back a lock of her dishevelled hair.

"I'm Jason Atkinson, and I'm running for state representative," I said in automode, handing her my palm card to deflect attention away from my intrusion.

"Yeah, yeah… I know who you are… I'm voting for you." She said dismissively. "I hear you work hard and aren't like those other politicians. Just… just make us proud."

"Thank you very much." I grinned, thinking I was off the hook, and about-faced myself off the porch but this woman wasn't quite through.

"Hey, wait a minute. I need you to do me a favor."

As I stopped short, and slowly turned around I thought, 'All the newspapers and self-interests are saying I'm going to lose this election in a few weeks and this lady is asking for constituent help?'

"Pardon me?" I said.

"I need you to come in the house and do me a favor!"

Now, you've probably already figured out that responding to a request of this nature is a pretty bad idea.

I'm pretty sure that there is a candidate instruction manual somewhere that cautions: When standing on a single woman's doorstep and she asks you to come in and do her a favor, KEEP WALKING!

For some reason I still don't quite understand, I decided to help. Before I knew it, we were upstairs near what must have been her kids' rooms, judging from the noise on the other side of the door.

"Mr. Atkinson, just stand right here and don't say a word when I open the door."

'This has got to be the weirdest public service request of all time.' I thought.

Standing with the door just inches from my nose, my shoulders nearly reached to both sides of the doorframe and my hair brushed the top of the door jam. *When this house was built a hundred years ago, people were smaller,* I nervously mused while thanking my lucky stars there were no newspaper photographers near by. They would have loved this shot.

"This is perfect," she grinned.

Behind the door, the "battle" raged. Things were hitting the walls. Voices of young boys yelled. Imaginary explosions were detonated. I could hear small feet stretching bedsprings while other voices laughed between yells.

All of a sudden, the lady reached past me, turned the knob, and threw the door open.

Two boys, arms cocked full of Legos stood horrified at the sight of this strange man, staring down at them, filling the entire doorframe. Their target, the third boy, stopped jumping on the bed as his face turned white. There was nowhere to hide.

The woman broke the silence.

"BOYS, THIS MAN'S FROM THE GOVERNMENT AND HE'S HERE TO INSPECT CLEAN ROOMS."

I fought back a smile as the boys gaped at me, jaws (and Legos) dropping. Looking each boy in the eye, I commanded, "You boys listen to your Mother and get this cleaned up. Don't make me come back here."

As I left the house, smiling and laughing to myself, she mouthed the words: "Thank You!"

Walking back to my truck, I began to realize that this woman had taught me more about Oregonians and public service than nearly any other single experience I have had.

And now, even eight years later as I run for governor, I think about what I learned that day: we want practical solutions for complex problems, solutions which don't rob us of our strength, our spirit, our independence.

People want to believe the substance of their public servants is deeper than a sound byte—that they care about more than just the next election. People want government to help when needed, but largely stay out of their way.

I can't stress too strongly that we are at a crossroads in this state with our children's education, our economy, health care, immigration control, and the misuse of political power.

You might expect a politician to say that change is needed! But I'm not saying that— because I don't need to. We live with the results of delayed budgets, the effects of unemployment, over-taxed families and businesses, and decisions which consistently take power away from the people of our state. Oregonians have a depressed feeling about our state and a belief we are headed in the wrong direction.

I am writing out of the conviction that solutions exist for these challenges, solutions that will strengthen our spirits, our independence. I am writing with the belief Oregon can be great again and our state can be turned in a new direction.

This small book is about the solutions. I'm inviting you to walk with me on a path where, together, we change our state.

IT REALLY SHOULD BE
ABOUT CHILDREN

I guess I must have done alright learning English because later, in high school, I was able to strike a deal with my friend Dave Wright: I'd get a ride to Mt. Ashland, our local ski resort, for each poem I helped him with. I spent hours in the coat closet at the Oregon Shakespeare Festival helping with Dave's homework while he worked as an usher. It worked great, until Dave started getting better scores in poetry than me!

I put myself through state college, acquiring a love for history and political science in the process. At one point my senior year, I was working at four jobs and remember the satisfaction of paying off all my school debt two weeks before I graduated. After several years pursuing professional sports, I returned to graduate school, working my way through again, and receiving an MBA.

By the time I began serving in the legislature, I figured my commitment to education was clear. As a Republican, I thought I could reach across the aisle, working also with legislators from that other party, to make education a priority.

Wasn't that clear? Education needs to be a real priority—not just an opportunity for good public relations. Politicians from all parties certainly can agree to that... right?

But I had to learn the hard way. There is a system, a game, a monopoly on education that sent me the message that, despite my experience at Southern Oregon State College and at Willamette University, I need not apply. Education in the Oregon Legislature is a game. This game is mostly about money and power. It is not about the needs of your children. I have to put it that bluntly because of a simple yet devastating tradition: Delaying the Education Budget for Political Power and Advantage.

Please stay with me and I guarantee you will be able to understand this. We must all understand this in order to help the children. Let me state it another way. The education needs of your children are the LAST consideration in the fight over the funding of education.

The largest budget item in our state (the one every politician says is *the priority* the K-thru-12 budget, is the last budget to pass. Why? Does it just turn out that way or is it a calculated political power play? The education budget in this state is about power politics. Period. I've heard of the first being last, but how is it that what everyone says is their first priority ends up being last?

Every other year the governor assembles a budget and reveals it in his *State of the State Address*. Here's how it works. The proposed K-thru-12 budget is purposely low. Self-interests from the education establishment send their lobbyists to the Capitol and stay hauntingly quiet for the first six weeks of the legislature. Then, like clockwork, on the Presidents' Day three-day holiday, busloads of kids are brought to the front steps of the capitol building to lobby the legislature. It makes for great television news reports and signals the beginning of the bidding war.

For the next five, six, and even *seven months* the legislature tries to "up" the Governor's budget, but time is ticking away. Instead of helping to pass the budget, the self-interests beg the legislature to delay, wait, wait, wait… until they see how the economy is doing (through an economic forecast) in hope of getting more money.

In the meantime, the legislature is passing less important budgets (i.e. spending money) while the education self-interests are pleading for delay. Their hope is that by running out the clock they can break legislators who don't agree with the numbers they have already proposed for the budget.

Most hard-working teachers and parents who are concerned with the education of their children have no idea how this "game" works — or that there is even a game being played. But, it is happening and is damaging the education of Oregon students and the credibility of state government. Education politics at the state level have a snowball effect across the state. The self-interests' delaying tactics create a guessing game in your local community. School boards are required to submit their budgets before state government gives them a final number. With school funding being tossed around the legislature in Salem like a football, they have to guess. Some guess low, and some high. Here's where the politics come in. I have watched some of my colleagues propose budget numbers for education that are not based in any sense on reality, but are proposed simply to make headlines. These legislators tell their school districts to propose an outrageously high number. Then, when the legislature finally passes the budget at a lower number, a number that is still higher than the governor's proposal, all self-interests fall in behind. And what do you think they do next? They call the budget a cut! One party is blamed for "cutting education," while the other presents itself as the protector of education. The governor, who set the bar low in the first place, walks away from the "budget battle" unscathed by any bad publicity.

In my first session in the legislature, the governor started his K-thru-12 budget at $4.4 billion and the legislature increased it by $400 million. Still, when I returned to my home at the close of the session, I discovered that the newspapers reported that I had *cut* education! Self-interests bashed me and several colleagues who are devoted to education were also bashed because they were from the wrong party. Leaders from one of the most prominent self-interest groups in Salem went ballistic when they found out that we had received phone calls of thanks from many of our friends (who are teachers and former teachers of mine, some rank-and-file union members) for standing up for education. I had to learn the hard way. With things the way they are right now the money games are overshadowing the education of our children. The accepted way of doing things in Salem has centered for too long around one word: DELAY.

Here are ten facts:

With things as they are, it's not about children, it's about money and political power.

Since 1999, K-thru-12 spending has increased nearly $1 billion dollars.

An average of 88% of each dollar coming to the classroom is spent on labor and retirement.

Regardless of economic forecasts, education spending is *always* increased.

Every teacher in the public school system is a member of the Union. The Union takes a portion of the teacher's check and nearly all the money collected for "political purposes" is spent to elect one party.

The Oregon legislature has no "end date." Unlike other states who are required to finish their budgets in 60 days (Washington, Idaho, Utah, Florida), in 2005, it took 208 days to pass the K-thru-12 budget.

Teachers feel under assault, morale is low, and not every teacher is partisan or accepting "delay" as the answer. Most don't even know about the game of delay.

From the department of education to self-interest groups, the legislative branch to the executive branch, no one is on the same page with the numbers they use to build or define a the education budget.

Elected legislators are "out-gunned" by the delay game from the moment they take the oath of office. Most K-thru-12 lobbyists as well as most reporters have been in the Capitol longer than any legislator serving.

The delay in the legislature hurts rural legislators financially because they must pay for housing away from their homes during session, while those from the metro area can commute.

There is a way of breaking this monopoly of self-interests and there is a way of fixing the political game of making education wait until last:

Fund education first!

Every politician in Salem will tell you that education is their #1 priority. Okay. Let's put our money where our mouth is. If elected governor, I will require the legislature to fund the K-thru-12 budget within the first one hundred days of the legislative session. End of story.

With this simple reform, there will be no incentive for future governors to put a falsely-low budget number forward. Future legislatures will have to start working hard in January, prioritize spending, and address education first. Self-interests will have to answer to a higher standard. Everyone will be required to use the same budget numbers. School boards across Oregon will know the funding level early and be able to build accurate local budgets on time. Instead of passing the budget somewhere in August, it will be done in three months. There is simply no reason for Oregon to delay any more.

These changes need to be made by constitutional initiative for two reasons. First, I want every Oregonian to know this is more than lip service; it's a mandate for the governor and for the legislative branch. Second, it should require a future constitutional mandate for future legislatures and future executives to change the rules. I know this will increase the power of the elected legislative branch, decrease the power of self-interests, and change when your tax money is spent. Most importantly, this action will build much-needed credibility with Oregonians who frankly do not believe the excuses they hear.

So why hasn't this happened already? It has been tried once. As a Senator, I introduced the "81-Day Bill" in 2005, a bill to force the passage of the education budget within 81 days. Immediately, I was characterized as not "getting it" and "not doing my time with the education establishment."

"What?" I thought, "Are these people serious?"

I know you expect responsive government. You have a right to expect it. We want our government back, we need legislators who don't just talk about education as a priority but who ACT based on what is best for the education of Oregon's children. "This is the way it's always been done" isn't good enough anymore. With legislative power organized to maintain the status quo, Oregon needs a governor with vision and the will to act in this matter. Funding K-thru-12 within 100 days is the first step.

Oregon public schools gave me a great start, and for that I am thankful. Let's see to it that Oregon's children have even better opportunities. Any well-practiced self-interest can incite outrage and get headlines, but Oregon wants more than "spend more money at the end." Oregon wants change. I know funding K-thru-12 within 100 days is the first step.

I want to live in an Oregon where we say, "It's not about money, it's not about political posturing and power, it's about kids and the first-rate education they deserve."

THE CAPITAL AND
THE COUCH

Serving in politics is not always that glamorous. In fact, working to keep my business going, serving as Senator, and keeping an active traveling and speaking schedule, has forced me many times to save money by sleeping at friends' houses around Oregon or on occasion sleeping overnight in my capitol office on my standard-issue-too-short-for-tall-senators-lengthwise-couch. Every time I do, I think of Abe, Lincoln the circuit-riding lawyer, bunking at friends' houses or Teddy Roosevelt under the stars in The Badlands trying to sort out if a public life was worth the cost.

There are some real hazards sleeping in the capitol. For instance, when the unsuspecting janitor, who has not seen a human being during the late night shift since Watergate, walks into my dark office with his Sony Walkman pumping and almost wets his pants went I sit up and instinctively yell at the top of my lungs, "HEY!"

After helping the poor victim off of the ceiling tiles, I try to convince him I am a senator just taking a nap between reviewing important policy papers affecting the future of the world.

I learned long ago to go out of my way to be kind to the janitors. I often sneak food out of the Senate lounge and leave it for the guys taking out the trash. I think a Pepsi and a cinnamon roll is the least I can do to say thanks for taking out all the trash my office can generate in a day.

Sneaking food out of the Senate lounge might not seem like that big of deal to you. But then again, you might not be a janitor and overlook the importance of caffeine and a sugar boost at 2:15am. But sneaking food is problematic, since I do not belong to the members-only lounge. I forgo my privileges.

There are a few reasons why. First is the price, second is my need to breathe air and take a walk outside away from the pressure cooker of the capitol during the noon hour, and third is, as a former athlete, I have a hard time eating the equivalent of Thanksgiving dinner each day. I still prefer a light lunch and a bike ride, thank you.

As I've thought about it, this is analogous to something happening in Oregon right now: a lot of people are working hard to hold it together, saving for the future, taking risks, and it could be argued that these are the very people who are sleeping unnecessarily on couches. Yet, during the last twenty years, state government has created a members-only belief that government knows better how to spend your money. Millions of dollars are locked up each year and those dollars are never released to the people who are doing all the work. It's called the "capital gains tax."

The capital gains taxation is a foolish, damaging tax. It is bad for our state in every way. It is the very reason that some of Oregon's wealthy individuals and successful businesses call Vancouver, Washington home. It also stands directly in the way of many who aren't wealthy and would just like to own a home. The capital gains tax robs us of jobs and opportunities.

In the 1980's, Oregon's capital gains tax rate was increased from 4.5 percent to 9 percent. Oregon won the notoriety of having the second highest capital gains tax rate in America — a title we still hold twenty years later.

If an Oregonian decides to make an investment for the future, say in property, in business, or even through buying stock, and then sells the investment at a profit, state government wants a big slice. After all, if you can afford to make an investment, the twenty-year-old way of doing things believes you are rich enough to pay a capital gains tax. In the same way, the fourth generation family farm that was passed down to you will be taxed. If it increases in value and you want to sell it, state government thinks it deserves a large slice of the increase.

The capital gains tax drives hardworking, productive citizens out of Oregon. A friend of mine called recently from Dallas, Texas. He excitedly told me how Texas didn't have Capital Gains and how easy the government was to work with. Incidentally, he also called to tell me he was relocating there, and taking his business with him. I wish this were a rare occurrence but there are many stories just like it.

After I gave a speech in Klamath Falls, a farmer came up to me and explained that he had asked his accountant for advice in passing the family farm on to his children. The accountant told him that, between Oregon's death tax and Capital Gains, he would be better off to make sure he died in Nevada.

Why are we giving a huge portion of our increase to the government? Does the government know better than you how to handle your money? Why are we allowing the government to confiscate the money we need to build our lives? What are we doing to ourselves?

Capital gains are thought of as a rich man's tax, but nothing could be further from the truth. More than half of the families in Oregon are subject to the Capital Gains Tax right now, and nearly 70 percent will be in their lifetime.

What if a family finally gets their fourth child off to college, wants to downsize their home and start a new business? The capital gains tax hits them right between the eyes. It is true that the first $500,000 isn't taxable but this is little comfort to the couple who are paying for their children's college and need to retire on the balance.

If a company purchases property to prepare for expansion of their business, and then decides to expand to the other side of town instead, and to sell the first property, they're hit with capital gains taxes.

Oregonians planning for retirement must, and do, plan around the tax to avoid capital gains. Millions upon millions of dollars are taken out of our state simply to avoid the taxes that the government will exact. Remove the tax and this money stays in Oregon and is put to work in Oregon creating jobs and building the economy.

Millions of dollars are locked up in the form of capital that no one can use to grow our economy. Instead of investing, hiring, buying and selling, expanding, and starting companies, each and every person who dreams a little has to plan their way around this tax.

Capital gains taxation should be called "Risk-Punishment Taxation" because that's what it is, and it punishes those who would normally take a little risk for growth — entrepreneurs, small businesses — the very people who drive Oregon's economy.

Imagine if settlers following the Oregon Trail knew when they arrived in Oregon and started a new life their investment risk was going to be taxed by state government. When they grew from their log cabin into the new white clapboard farmhouse, they'd have to pay the tax. (Somebody would likely have been tarred and feathered!) Is there any difference in modern Oregon? At the time I write, Oregon still struggles with unemployment, uncertain private property rights, and a twenty-year-old steadfast death-grip on keeping capital gains taxes in place. Don't you think Oregon's economy could do better?

In the biennial report of the Governor's Small Business Council of Oregon, the council concluded,

> "… *many successful Oregon business owners move to Washington, or other states, prior to selling their business, to avoid a tax of 9% or more on their gain. Once they are a resident of another state, they are less likely to reinvest in Oregon. The state should support modifications in tax policies that*

*encourage investment and reinvestment in Oregon
companies. For many small business owners, their
business is their primary asset, and also their
'retirement fund.'"*

Since I have been serving in the Oregon legislature,
I have been calling for the complete *elimination* of capital gains taxes in order to free up people's investments,
and get our economy rolling again.

In 2001, we had a tremendous push to reduce capital
gains taxes from nine percent back to four and a half percent. The harder we pushed, the louder the critics
squealed. These critics calculated that the state would lose
millions of dollars in revenue in the short term. Our
research showed $30 million dollars would not be brought
into the state government that year, but $180 million in
annual long-term investment capital would be freed up in
Oregon. Unfortunately, the critics still won, and the tax
continues to cripple Oregon.

Capital gains taxation hurts you and it hurts
Oregon, and the executive branch and the legislative
branch need to take responsibility to free Oregon of the
burden this tax creates.

I believe fundamentally in home ownership, allowing people to take business risk, and the value that comes

through hard work and planning. State government needs to help Oregonians succeed, not stand in their way. Today, Oregon has a Sears and Roebuck Catalogue state government in an eBay world. Oregon needs a new direction and we need to get our tax structure fixed. Unlocking the vast amount of capital in this state will unlock our potential to become the kind of state people won't move away from, but will stay instead and invest, build, and benefit from more growth.

A MEXICAN-AMERICAN

Have you ever eaten a hand-rolled tortilla right off a cast iron skillet? Do you know how to fold it so the warm butter doesn't drip out the bottom?

My "uncle" Art showed me.

In fact, I had to call Art Quesada "Uncle Art" before his wife, Rachel, would give me another tortilla. Art was Mexican, Rachel was Puerto Rican. Both were Americans and were my parents' closest friends.

I remember the big Sunday dinners, with all their family, proud immigrants, first generation Americans, second generation Americans, who had the Atkinson family over for "color." I didn't know any difference. I remember Luther, Uncle Art's brother, bringing a young man to church who escaped the Marxists in Central America. He wanted a new life, and the Quesadas helped him.

This country should be about helping people in ways that empower them to become strong citizens. I've seen this at work and it is beautiful.

However, there is a twin crisis over immigration that has been brewing for years, hurting our economy and affecting the rights of everyone.

First, in Oregon, it is easy for an illegal alien to obtain a driver's license. There is also a constant effort to allow illegals to vote, while non-emergency health care is easy to obtain at your — the taxpayer's — expense. It is perfectly reasonable that Oregonians are now asking, "Why is this happening?" Basic fairness dictates that we not spend taxpayer money to pay for services for citizens of other countries. Those taxes were collected to pay for the services needed by citizens of Oregon. Nothing is more common than politicians sidestepping this issue, but the sidestepping must stop.

But, there is another issue. How are we going to come to grips with the fact that our lack of immigration policy creates an incentive for illegal aliens to take advantage of the situation? It's clear that we discourage and devalue American citizenship through free handouts.

The problem is much wider than campaign sound bytes. In Oregon, employers do not have a quick and reliable way to verify if an employee is legal or illegal. There is an industry of creating forged documents that our state government and federal government have not addressed. If an employer sees an ID and sends in verification to social security, it takes up to five weeks to verify the numbers. If the numbers don't match up, the employer is in violation. If the employer suspects an ID is forged, but cannot prove it and denies employment, he faces a discrimination lawsuit. Truly, Oregon employers lose in both cases.

The other problem is the fact our border is still open and deportation has not been enforced, while it's easy to obtain an ID and open bank accounts in the U.S. This has built an underworld that is healthy for neither the American economy nor the non-Americans.

Accusations run rampant and tempers rage whenever the word 'amnesty' is mentioned. I do not support amnesty or a blanket pardon for people who have broken our laws. We are a nation of laws, and laws must be followed and respected.

Many Americans are angry about the suggestion that a guest-worker program will benefit America. I believe a guest-worker program, without amnesty, is a first step to stopping the incentive to break our immigration laws. There must also be reliable border enforcement, which is the first step to stopping illegal aliens from being hired, and the best way to take control of a situation we created ourselves.

Clearly, as "guests", those who want to come into America temporarily would not be entitled to vote, nor receive many of the services that come with citizenship. However, their rights would be protected under laws which would remove the present ambiguities and benefit everyone. At the same time, those guest workers that may want to become citizens would be given a clear path, which would require a clear commitment on their part.

The political left wants blanket amnesty. The political right wants deportation. But both of these arguments do not add up. Can you imagine the message blanket amnesty sends to the world during our war against terrorists? On the other side, can you imagine sending the National Guard door to door, rounding people up, and deporting them? I don't want to allow governmental eyes looking suspiciously at everyone with brown skin.

I live 90 miles from Tulelake, where Japanese American's were rounded up and imprisoned during World War II. I know America will not go back to that degree of paranoia, but we must be careful not to base any of our responses to such an emotional issue on race.

If you think America could snap its fingers and all illegal aliens would be gone, you may want to think again, because under that scenario, the economy would simply stop. There is a balance we must address as a state and as a nation. A balance between American values, compassion, respect for the laws, and undoing years of uncertainty.

So what about the illegal aliens already in the country? Above all, I do not believe in the angry rhetoric I hear so often. In most cases, the reason illegal immigrants are here is that America promises a better life and our porous laws allow them to take advantage. Although I understand this, I still believe in enforcing the rule of law and do not believe in pardons for illegal activity.

Will illegal aliens have to leave America and apply legally? Perhaps. Will they pay a hefty fine or face deportation? Perhaps. This will be the federal debate the President of the United States will broker in 2006. There is nothing any governor of the fifty states can do other than declare a border emergency, enforce the immigration laws the states have on the books, stop state services from being taken advantage of and stop the incentive to break the law.

After September 11, 2001, America changed and protecting our homeland became the national issue. (As I write, there is a pending court case concerning an illegal alien, who was extradited to England, who had earlier been attempting to establish an Al-Qaeda training camp in the remote southeastern Oregon town of Bly.) This issue is real and it is not directed at just one nationality. Federal immigration policy is not consistent at present and this must be improved. We must also improve the ways we maintain security.

I support enforcing all of our borders as a matter of national security. I support giving employers an instantaneous way of verifying if an employee is legal or illegal. As governor, I will stop drivers' licenses from being given to illegal aliens, stop the push to allow for illegal aliens to vote, and stop non-emergency health care to illegal aliens at the taxpayer's expense.

I believe it is time for Oregon to change direction. We must acknowledge that our policies have been wrong. We can't afford to keep going in this direction. We need to get back to balance, fairness, and respect for the taxpayer. I believe Oregonians, immigrants, and our communities need certainty, consistency, and fairness in our immigration policy and a federal policy that helps agriculture, not that hurts people.

Finally, this debate should treat the needs of human beings with dignity and compassion. That's what a well-regulated guest-worker system will promote. People, legal or illegal, should not be exploited for their labor without regard to their needs. Employers should not be able to hire illegal immigrants and keep people in the shadows.

The time has come for the federal government to provide Oregon with a well-regulated guest-worker program and a more clear and fair route to citizenship for those who will commit to it. All of this adds up to respect for the laws of the land.

Let's not forget that America is a nation of immigrants—immigrants who are hard working, responsible, risk-taking, community-minded people. Our present way of living with illegal aliens is not, ultimately, any help to them nor is it any help to building a stronger state and nation.

I found an example of the strength immigrants bring when I was talking to some Russian immigrants who are now legal Oregonians. They had fled their homeland to escape Marxist religious persecution, had applied for citizenship, and now are part of a Russian community in Oregon that is strong. They are proud and productive Americans. They understand the commitment it takes to become an American citizen and want immigration laws upheld. They also have a heart for people, which I believe is one element that is needed in this national debate.

Recently I received an email from a kind gentleman who told me he was finishing the process of immigrating legally to America and that I would be the first person for whom he had ever voted. I was stunned and humbled.

Here was a proud man who followed his dream, immigrated, was successful and proud of his work, started a family, and was about to be given the title he wanted more than any other: American. And he wanted me to become his Governor.

"Uncle" Art smiled on me that day.

As citizens of the greatest country on earth, as Americans, we still live in the most desirable and free society on earth. We are not giving hopeful immigrants any favors or providing a hand-up when our immigration laws are weak and full of politically correct holes.

If you are looking for conventional solutions or political rhetoric, I'm not your man. In order to effectively address this serious problem, creativity is essential and we must always respect the basic dignity of every person.

The day she said yes!

A happy moment in the 2003 legislative
session. Perry has freshly out of the hospital.

Days when my family visit the Capitol are always
exciting and in motion.

After going through a windshield
and going into politics, I started
racing again in 2004 and winning..

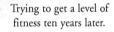
Trying to get a level of
fitness ten years later.

Racing in Europe in US colors.

I always liked this picture. We were joking about a mutual friend before he spoke to a crowd of thousands.

Taken during a trip to China. I have been blessed to travel and experience other cultures.

جلالة الملك يستقبل وفد المجلس الأمريكي لقادة المؤسسين الشباب
His Majesty Receives the delegation of ACYPL

Traveling in Jordan, I was given an audience with His Majesty King Abdullah.

My brother took this on our home hill, Mt. Ashland.

Long after politics are over for me,
I'll still chase my favorite fish with Spey Rods!

My son and I on the steps
at the Capitol in 2005.

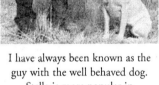

I have always been known as the
guy with the well behaved dog.
Stella is more popular in
hunting circles than I am. At least
she lets me come with her!.

My second grade teacher
and principal visiting me
in the Senate Chambers.

My Steph and my Pomp.

Pomp's First Fish
caught with the help
of his Mother.

CHANGE THE ETHIC
ONE CAST AT A TIME

I got up at dawn with Stella (my faithful yellow lab) and we headed out to talk to a few ducks.

It was a needed break in a very busy campaign schedule in the fall of 2005. I had been to Portland, Hood River, Pendleton, Kimberly, Mt. Vernon, and Prineville. My family met me in Bend, re-charged me with clean laundry (and dropped off Stella) and then I drove to Silver Lake, Summer Lake, Paisley and Plush. Then I had a few hours to myself.

It was about 5 degrees, no wind, and the water was all frozen in the Warner Valley. My search for open water and some unsuspecting ducks stopped after a few hours and I ended up at the top of the National Antelope Refuge where I knew there was a hot spring. Snow capped peaks, and snow dust still in the shadows, steam rose off my bath as I realized only in Oregon could a guy like me, campaigning for governor, stop to find such inspiring beauty.

So, not seeing a soul, I stripped off my wet waders, warm parka and sweater, and hopped in. It was perfect. I sat in my natural hot tub, grinning, satisfied, and thinking about the campaign.

I got up, steamed dry in the frozen air and had just barely pulled on my essentials when I turned around to find that I wasn't alone.

"Where'd you come from?" I asked startled and embarrassed.

"'Round there!" he said pointing to a clump of trees, "Who are you?"

"I'm Jason Atkinson."

"Jason Atkinson?" a long puzzled look overtook him before his forehead crinkled and he looked up at me, "Aren't you…?"

"Yeah, I'm running for governor."

He grinned, started to laugh, and had to say something.

"You mean to tell me I just missed seeing the next governor of Oregon half naked?"

I smirked and said, "No sir, you just missed seeing the next governor of Oregon all naked."

But I am not at all embarrassed to be completely exposed on where I see solutions to today's issues—including the environment. In a nutshell, I am a Republican who cares about the environment, believes in the goodness of people, and loves the company of gun-dogs in drift boats and duck blinds. I want to leave it better than I found it, which means tackling some big issues with action, not talk.

When I was first elected to the House of Representatives, I wrote an op-ed for the Oregonian about the historical differences in the word 'conservation', and how the Republican Party must return to its Theodore Roosevelt / Gifford Pinchot roots. I argued to "manage, protect, and restore." I wanted to write a wake up call to my party to get engaged and take back a set of issues.

Was I disappointed!

Never before or since, have I received so much hate mail. Anonymous mail showed up calling me every name in the book. Letters were written bashing me personally, bashing Republicans, and asserting that the only way to protect the environment was to keep people out of it. These angry critics had no room for the middle. They cited lawsuits and examples in other countries of environmental abuse and how they were the only thing stopping that same pillaging from happening in Oregon. Finally, when one critic used my op-ed as toilet paper and sent it to me in protest, I realized it was not worth having my wife open the mail anymore.

But labels don't manage, protect, and restore, people do. Now, years later, I know the debate over Oregon's many environmental issues has less to do with progress and more to do with having an example to incite fear and to raise money to keep non-governmental organizations going.

I believe we need to strive for the cleanest, richest, most sustainable environment possible—not because nature is some sort of god we can't touch, but because ethical living demands it. My goal is to protect, manage, and improve our environment. I believe a balance is possible between using the environment (which we need to do to stay alive) and nourishing it so that it can be used by generations to come. We can all agree that destruction isn't ultimately good for any economy! But I also think it's foolish to ignore the fact that everyone concerned about the environment is making an impact on it. Isn't the point to make sure we make that impact wisely, in as economically-freeing way as possible, keeping the long view in mind? It's about wading into the issues, living responsibly with both the environment and our present and future needs.

First, the big picture. I believe our state needs to get more serious about recycling than it already is. Yes, we have recycling. Yes, people's awareness and practice is growing. But we need to look at how recycling can better stimulate the economy—how it can help grow businesses in this state. I believe we are only at the beginning of this journey. Recycling is underutilized in part because it needs to make more sense to the business community.

Years ago, Oregon was seen by the world as a leader in alternative energy innovation. I'm referring in part to our world famous wood-burning stove designs which drastically reduced particulate emission. It is time for us to reclaim this heritage. Let's face it: the world needs solutions. We can all agree that we don't want our children breathing polluted air or suffering from an increase in ultra-violet radiation. Surely, Oregon, with its technological know-how and innovation heritage can continue to make a contribution.

You cannot talk about the environment without talking about land-use planning. Over thirty years ago Oregon captured the nation's attention with the creation of state-wide land-use planning. Unfortunately, today, the debate surrounding centralized planning is ripping Oregon in half: urban vs. rural.; farm vs. city.; voters vs. self-interests. People are frustrated, the rules are hard to follow and many times hard for governments to justify, and property rights will be decided by courts after years of delay and appeal. If we are serious about the environment, we must be serious about property rights.

Now let me tell you what I've already been able to do to step towards these goals.

Despite all the politics inside the Capitol, I will love my river and chasing waterfowl with wet nosed warm-hearted dogs long after my days in politics are over. To that end, I have made Republicans nervous and Democrats sceptical by pushing through legislation my son will point to with pride.

I worked closely with the Warm Springs Reservation to allow them to grow Salmon and Steelhead in the same manner I saw on our river as a boy. I was again called every name in the book by critics and got my first taste of shuttle diplomacy negotiating between tribal elders in the Capitol's basement café and the Oregon Department Fish and Wildlife (ODFW) leaders in the first floor hallway. In the end, notwithstanding a federal mandate, we allowed Oregon tribes to keep their practice in place, put more fish in the river, and got the entire legislature to bless the union with unanimous votes in both chambers!

A friend of mine and I were chasing fish, and occasionally getting the eye over by a few curious bears on the Russian River in Alaska, when I learned of a unique fishing tackle recycling program. I introduced the Keep Oregon Rivers Clean Act the next legislative session to test the concept on six Oregon rivers. Working in concert with the

ODFW, local sportsman groups, conservation groups, and other local "friends" groups would place fish tackle cleanup containers at popular fishing spots and boat take outs. The issue is the monofilament line, fluorocarbon line, and lead. Not only do these clog rivers and scar fish, but they also greatly damage birds that either get tangled in the stuff or attempt to build nests out of it.

All I want to do is change the ethic. Just like some who supported the Bottle Bill a generation before, I wanted to keep our rivers clean and allow a kid and his grandpa, (or grandma in my case) to pick up and pass on to a coming generation the ethic of conservation.

Well it worked! In fact, it worked better than I ever expected. From steelheaders to the Audubon Society, from friends of fish hatcheries to fly-fishing clubs, groups who do not always see eye to eye were working together. We took the program statewide, to all rivers, and the effect has been great.

Oregon's National Park, Crater Lake National Park, had its centennial and the event got under my skin. If Teddy Roosevelt could start it one hundred years ago, then Senator Atkinson was going to do his part. The Oregon Crater Lake license plate was born and all the excess proceeds go to the National Park Trust to rebuild the Science and Learning Center and provide a program for school kids using the Park as their classroom. To date, it has been an extremely popular license plate and program, a tremendous success. My grandfather would be proud.

When I was a freshman lawmaker, I worked to pass a law to have the representation of the Land Conservation and Development Commission regionalized. Instead of most the Commission being from one part of the state, I wanted each congressional district to have a representative. I believe strongly in regional planning and regional representation to make the rules. What makes sense in Baker City doesn't necessarily make sense in Coos Bay. Likewise, the planning ideas which work in Beaverton in many cases do the exact opposite in Southern Oregon. I have seen the best farmland paved while much less valuable land, that will never be farmed, protected.

My first step at regional planning worked, but it was only a first step.

Recently, a lobbyist who vigorously supports land-use planning admitted to me personally, that after 30 years of administrative rules and laws, the land-use system we have today in Oregon is designed to break people emotionally and financially.

If you had ever worked with a farmer who was being encroached upon by a city and wanted to rezone, and had seen him in tears as he told how he spent $25,000 on lawyer's bills, received different answers from the city, county, and state government and finally decided to leave Oregon, your heart would break.

Our land-use planning system has become a burden to the lifestyles we want to protect and a maze of "hide the ball" politics for those who want to navigate the system.

I believe strongly in having a land-use system in which the rules are easy to understand. When the above-mentioned farmer asked me, his Senator, for help, the city, the county, and the state all had different interpretations of the law and a different timeline to get answers.

Property rights are the backbone of what makes the American economy work. Any time property rights are uncertain, any time a right is threatened to be taken away, it has a ripple effect on home ownership, employment, and the credibility of governments, not to mention the environment.

Thirty years from now, I want Oregon to still have valuable farms, our cities to have the ability to expand on less valuable land, for property owners to be able to build without years of lawsuits, and a known-quantity of quality locations for business to expand. I want to have communities in Oregon. I believe in the power of the small town. I also believe in the power of local people to make long-term decisions locally.

"That's nice, but it's not enough." is the comment I always get from the environmental extreme. On the other side, a Democratic friend of mine said something nice about me in the newspaper, and a lobbyist from the timber industry thought I had secretly sold them out. Sometimes I wonder: *"Is the hassle it worth it?"* Well, it is. All the controversy will go away when I am an old man standing in a river pleading with a steelhead for one little ride.

Oregon has huge issues to tackle, but it all starts with the ethic of manage, protect, and restore. Apart from a common ground, we are only employing lawyers.

The Willamette River is a nationally recognized Super-fund, (or, more aptly, a disaster) site. Having the residents of Portland put up the money for a new sewage system, preventing sewer run-off from going into the river, is a giant first step. I believe the next step is to finish the job and scour the years of pollution out of the harbor area. But we must first give river-side landowners protection and an incentive to clean it up. Lawsuits make people rich, but don't get salmon up the river.

I am interested in the concept of Environmental Justice, the issue of Oregon's most poor living in the place with the dirtiest environment. To that end, Oregon will know the Willamette is clean when a kid from northeast

Portland can spend a day fishing on the Willamette in his own neighbourhood.

The same is true upstream. We can either have a hostile view of agriculture, put agricultural polluters out of business through sets of regulation and threats of lawsuits, or we can partner together. After eight years of these battles, seeing very little progress on the big picture, I do believe it all starts with the ethic of conservation and working with people.

The Willamette's flyway is not healthy. Canadian geese have found what Oregon's first settlers found, a tremendously abundant dreamland, and they don't move on. Instead, they winter in Oregon, destroying crops. All the while waterfowl (the indicator species I pay a lot of attention to) numbers are down. While Oregon is negotiating with native tribes in Alaska (who use the goose for subsistence and who want a greater take) and while the U.S. is working with Canada for waterfowl production, the environment is not in balance. I strongly believe in greater incentives for habitable restoration and long-term investments to manage Oregon's bird, game, and fish populations.

Oregon's government was formed to handle the dissolution of a personal estate and to handle a cougar predation problem. While estate law has been established in modern Oregon, the next ten years will force wolf and cougar issues to the forefront once again. While I do not support the introduction of wolves into Oregon and do support management of the cougar population, I believe Oregon's government must move away from species-dependant debates and move toward habitat debates. (The spotted owl taught us all a lot, but its most beaming lesson seems to be that people are important and that lawsuits divide.) Oregon must also address the environmental problems of the Pacific Shore. Communities on the Oregon Coast depend on the health of the marine environment. I am willing to work to find ways to manage the rock fishery and the communities that depend on the ocean for survival.

In the last twenty years the timber industry in Oregon has slowed to a crawl due to lawsuits by radical environmentalists. The timber managers are stymied by court rulings and cases pending. The courts now decide what timber can go and what can stay. It is clear that the courts are not the right places to manage forests, yet the forests must be protected. I have been blessed to travel to Asia and Africa, and have seen first hand how their forest practices are destroying their countries. I have tried to run in Tiananmen Square during a dust storm kicked up by strip logging a thousand miles away. I have seen teak forests destroyed in West Africa that will not grow back in my lifetime. Three times in three different countries , my hosts (when they found out I was from Oregon) asked me how to get help from Oregon State University's forestry program. Our international reputation in Forest Science is sterling.

Yet in Oregon, our rural communities are slowed by wrong policies. Forests are managed with prices set to compensate for threatened lawsuits and the hassle of delay. America's largest forest fire in 2002 was the Biscuit Fire in my district. My office organized neighbor-to-neighbor relief for families and their livestock, and support for the fire fighters. Who knows how many 4-H animals Cheri, my long-time legislative assistant, saved. But once the smoke cleared, Oregon saw the timber debate first-hand. Rough and Ready saw mill, across the street from the Biscuit complex, could not salvage logs. These logs lay on the ground, during months, then years of lawsuits and delays, until they had little salvage value. Workers in the mill would call my office and ask me, "isn't there anything you can do?"

The fact was, I couldn't. As Senator, I was forced to wait under the system of delay and watched hard-working Oregonians placed on unemployment. While some just thought it was another news story, people in Oregon were hurting.

These people, Oregon's timber workers, are sportsmen too. I have never met one timber worker who was not proud of their stewardship of the forest. But they were being put out of work by an ineffective government in favor of wood from other countries whose forest policies are in fact destroying their own natural environments. Is this ethical?

There is a balance of protecting the last great forests of Oregon and managing a renewable resource based on world-class science that keeps our communities healthy.

So where is the balance? We know it's not in waiting for Washington D.C. to adopt better fuel efficiency standards for automobiles or putting a twenty-five year old California emission standard in place in Oregon. The only effect of that is to provide an election issue and to jack up the new truck price for a rancher in Burns by three thousand dollars. The answer isn't more lawsuits.

The balance starts with people—real people. People need five things to take care of their environment:

The first is a job. With a job comes homeownership, then pride in community, then pride in our state. Does that sound too simplistic? Find me one unemployed Oregonian who is renting and trying as hard as they know to hold it all together and ask them how interested they are in closing down a sawmill or paying more for gas.

Second, the balance starts with the ethic. Democrats, Republicans, Independents, Greens, non-voting disenfranchised just-leave-me-alone Oregonians think twice before tossing trash out their car window on I-5 or using the recycle bin. The point is, the ethic in America has changed, and we can do more. My son will not litter fishing line, and I bet yours will not either.

The third thing is that people need to see some action happen. Talk is cheap and lawsuits are expensive. The Willamette Harbor area needs legislation to protect landowners, and gives clean-up incentives. This is America's river and Oregon's pride, but it needs immediate, concentrated action. The harbor area in Portland needs to be restored and the water cleaned. It's a mess. Let's clean it up.

Fourth, people need to know we are in this together. The environment cannot be improved without farmers and ranchers. Period. The ranching and farming communities have changed dramatically and are now competing in a world market. We need cattlemen's know how, modern agricultural practices, and landowners. If Oregonians really care about the environment, they must first care about farmers and ranchers.

Fifth, Oregonians must live in 'today'. The environment is better today than it was in the 1970's. The old rhetoric is hurting our national reputation and our economy. Statewide our rivers are cleaner. Our private timber management sets the international standard for excellence. Fish runs are coming back. Sure we have our challenges and issues to fight for, but Oregon has come a long way. Our greatest days were not in the 1970's; they are part of our tomorrow. Keeping rivers clean, the fish coming back, and managing wildlife for the long term is second nature. My grandparents expected it of me, and it is how I will govern.

My grandmother is a liberal Democrat and proud of it, I might mention. Even though she always is supportive and encouraging to me, she seems to always get jabs in about "your party" and "you'll join me one day." My grandfather was a quiet Eisenhower Republican. A do-your-part, give-something-back, you-owe-it-to-America kind of man. Spending summers with them on the porch, watching the river, the only area they agreed on was the environment.

We used to take day-trips to watch native tribes raise steelhead in creeks and do our part to pick up trash, open culverts for fish, and occasionally catch river trout and give them an all-expenses-paid trip to our pond. Then I would "test" various fly patterns I had tied on the pond fish. The problem was, the fish got on to me quickly. No band-aid across their tried lips could repair our relationship.

We would debate the Carter administration, the air traffic controller's strike, the artistic importance of *The Thornbirds* mini-series, Iran/Contra, the strategic defense initiative and whether or not Luke loved Laura. I was not much for the latter controversy, but time moves slower on the river. I became a debater on that porch at my grandparents', learning to hold my own, form opinions, and think on my feet. But the environment, keeping the river clean, the fish coming back, and managing wildlife for the long term was second nature. It was expected. You're an Atkinson, you do your part.

My grandfather was a founding member of *Ducks Unlimited*. My Dad is an accomplished sportsman, who at one time had a fishing show on television. My grandmother hunted deer. (This tiny little liberal carried a 30.06!) The ethic is: take care of it, manage it, protect it, and respect it. Today, my son is the fifth generation to sit on that porch and chase steelhead in "our river."

Natural Oregon is to be loved, protected, and given away to our kids. Whether a cold duck blind, an urban river, a small community who depends on timber, a commercial fisherman, or people like my grandparents who want to pass on the ethic. Oregon is the most beautiful place in the world and it is ours to protect.

METHAMPHETAMINES
AND HOPE

L inda and I became acquainted as adversaries. I wanted to help a business in Hood River grow, she was helping a business in Central Oregon, and we clashed over an archaic land-use law that made sense in the Willamette Valley, but made heads ache everywhere else.

Linda is the former Mayor of Sisters, former Deschutes County Commissioner, and occasionally takes on projects at the Capitol for the resort community. After we compromised, and started working together, I felt there was something special about Linda.

"Why do you do this?"

"Well Senator Atkinson, this is how I pay my bills and keep Bridges to Hope going."

Bridges to Hope, I found out that day, is a non-profit, faith-based, organization Linda founded to help women transition from prison to society. Bridges to Hope takes women, many of whom have had a past that would stifle most imaginations, and gives them future.

Bridges to Hope identifies these women, some before they even get out, and simply loves them. They befriend them. Over time, education is organized for each woman, they help former prisoners become productive, responsible, and caring members of society. The counselors share their faith. Many of these women have never felt unconditional love before. Through horrible personal stories of abuse, unemployment, and broken families, many had turned to drugs, which eventually lead to prison.

I became intrigued. Each time Linda would come into my office to talk land-use, I wanted to talk about Bridges to Hope. The stories of these women inspired me.

A few weeks passed, and Linda was back at my office, this time with a few women from the program. I seated them in my office and decided to talk "land-use" quickly to get the business of government out of the way before I started to listen to heart-wrenching stories of my guests. Each time, I found myself overcome with emotion as they told me how they ended up behind bars, feeling trapped by their lifestyle, and how one person at Bridges to Hope made a connection with them and now they were on a new path. These women were different. They felt forgiven. They felt new. They were excited about their futures, many for the first time in their lives. Listening to them was like having open-heart surgery in one instant and being overcome with pride the next.

Then one day, Linda brought a woman in to see me that changed everything.

Linda walked in with an arm full of bills, notes, and amendments, and in tow was a woman about my age, with beautiful facial features and hair, but whose skin was worn. She was nervous to see me and walked closely behind Linda. Even though it was warm in Salem that spring day, she wore long sleeves. Her eyes were a warm blue, but guarded a fear and former hollowness. Let's call her Susan.

Susan was just out of solitary confinement and recently paroled to Linda's care. During her first parole, Susan cut off her ankle bracelet, used to keep track of prisoners on home-release, and sought out another fix of methamphetamine. Out of work, without a home, and hooked on meth, she evaded capture for parole violation for six weeks. Susan's arms had scars from her attempts at other drugs. Her face was worn. Her skin was thin and broken from the years of meth. But, as she told me her story, how Bridges to Hope rescued her, how she had been off drugs for the first five months since she was a teenager, and how her new faith gave her a reason to walk forward, she began to cry.

My heart broke too. So much for "Mr. Senator", all three of us were reaching for the Kleenex.

Many of the bills, issues, laws, and government we talk about in Salem are void of the ability to help women like Susan. Government can stiffen penalties, create education programs, and expand health care, but it cannot become someone's friend. Government can fill a lot of roles, but it cannot fill a broken heart.

Oregon has a tremendous methamphetamine problem. Meth is cheap, highly addicting, and easy to make with over-the counter medications. Using pseudoephedrine, an ingredient found in common cold-medications, thousands of dollars worth of methamphetamine can be created. In 2005, the Oregon legislature became the national leader in fighting meth—pseudoephedrine is now regulated and meth-makers can't get the huge quantities over the counter. Local law enforcement has been given the tools to combat meth and the industry of identity theft, and more tools for treatment have been created to help people get off this terrible drug. Will this series of reforms end meth in Oregon? No. However, it will greatly slow down production in Oregon, driving the price of meth up, reducing its availability.

But what about people like Susan? They are hooked and hopeless. If you think about it, you know a "Susan." These are our friends, the people we knew in high school, the people who live in the next town, or around the corner. These are the people we don't like to look at, who we easily pigeon hole into "them" and who we don't like to talk about. But we all know who they are.

Now ask yourself: what is government's role? Let's drill down, below the surface of politics, and look for real reasons why Oregonians get caught in this sticky web which leads to prison. If we were to profile most meth users, we would find most are unemployed, between ages of 22 and 42, with little post-high school education, and from broken families.

Drug use rises with unemployment. Oregon, for the past six years, has lead, or has been in America's top three, states with the highest employment. Even while other states with less economic diversity grew out of recession and the post 9-11 economy, Oregon has been stuck. The small business climate is difficult, land-use laws are uncertain, and the general feeling in the business community is "Oregon is an unfriendly place to do business." We talk about attracting new business, but more have left. Small rural communities, once the center of timber production in America, are hurting and have become the center of meth production.

We can fix this. We can be "pro-business" again, but need an entirely new attitude coming from state government. I want a state government that asks, "What can we do to help you" rather than "I wonder how you fit into our regulations?" Being pro-business is more than lip service. We need real change. Oregon needs to grow our Oregon business with incentives to invest. State government must cut regulations and stop passing all costs off on small business. State government must lead the way, and agencies's attitudes must change. To paraphrase Winston Churchill, Oregon's making it difficult for business to grow is like a man standing in a bucket and trying to lift himself up by the handle.

Oregon can put people to work, but old political ideas keep people on government assistance. Each legislative session, the state bureaucracy fights, waters down, and tries to stop a concept called Jobs Plus. Jobs Plus is a welfare, unemployment and food stamp replacement concept that converts benefits to wage subsidies for transitional, training-oriented, predominantly private sector jobs. Even with modest and watered down implementation of Jobs Plus, Oregon has experienced significant declines in welfare caseloads, while saving money and placing people in long term jobs, many of which have been well in excess of the minimum wage. Why wouldn't Oregon fully embrace putting people to work?

Would life have been different if Susan had a job and the self-pride that comes from work? Would life have been different if Susan could afford to go to college in Oregon? Would life have been different if Susan could afford to be a homeowner?

Life would have been different if Susan did not come from a broken family, but she did. Government can do very little to keep people in love or force parents to be responsible, but Philanthropic Oregon can. Each year, millions of private dollars are spent as non-profits, faith-based organizations, churches, and private relief programs help Oregonians in need. Instead of embracing the help, the attitude in Salem is "keep faith and service separate" and "that's nice, but we have our own agency for that, and by the way it needs more money."

The Grants Pass Gospel Rescue Mission and the Gospel Rescue Mission on Burnside in downtown Portland do not use government funds, but they fill a role government cannot.

Lives are changed.

Sparrows Clubs reach in and help kids in medical crisis and change the hearts of once-selfish students into servants. It works.

Bridges to Hope, Friends of the Children, and Oregon Mentors, all make a countless difference in the lives of lonely and hurting Oregonians.

Why not have state government and Philanthropic Oregon work together? I believe in building strong creative partnerships between state government, Philanthropic Oregon, and the faith communities to work together. After all, aren't we all in public service for the same reason?

I went into public service because I was attracted to the idea government can do good for people. Government can provide opportunity and freedom for citizens. I enjoy moving big ideas on the public stage. But my experience with a former meth user changed me. How can I, how can state government, and how can we Oregonians give someone like Susan a hand up?

First, we have to give the Susans every opportunity to work. Second, we have to give every available opportunity for people to get an affordable world-class education, either vocational or academic, and have the self-respect that come with learning. Third, Oregonians must be able to become homeowners. Fourth, our streets have to be safe from drugs, sexual predators, and the like. Law enforcement must be given every available tool instead of being punished by the legislature. Fifth, our tax policies must allow Oregon to grow again. Capital gains taxes must be eliminated. When our economy is healthy, Oregon state government will have more tax revenue. (It's not the other way around.)

Finally, faith is a good thing. Faith, private philanthropy, and private programs to help people in need work, change lives, and provide the friendship and self-worth government simply cannot. We should work together, because we are in this together.

CHARACTER DRIVEN
POLITICS

Our hometown, despite redistricting, is Jacksonville. Our church is the oldest church in Jackson County, originally established by a circuit rider, with stained glass that came around South America by ship and was carried by wagon train to where they are now. The town was the center of the Gold Rush in Oregon for a few years. As strange as this sounds, I do not believe Oregon's gold rush is over. I wouldn't be running for governor if I didn't believe there is hidden in this state the resources to overcome our greatest challenges.

When I say "resources" I am speaking of the character of Oregonians. The resources of the character of our people, the resources of quality work, the resources of being independent, and the resources of faith.

The problem is public service has lost credibility in recent years, and Oregonians feel a disconnect from what is perceived as just more "politics as usual."

It is my goal in this chapter to let you know about a resource which, if nourished, mined, and set free by a new direction, could radically transform our state, as it did a generation ago.

In 1954, Senator John F. Kennedy was recovering from back surgery, and wrote about a topic he was fascinated with: political courage. His book, *Profiles in Courage* was later published and highlighted the political bravery of eight Senators who, by standing on their principle of what was best for the country, took tremendous risk, voted and spoke their conscience. Many lost future political position, lost the favor of their party's faithful, and some, like Sam Houston of Texas, lost his job. However, as American history records, their bravery shaped the country we have today.

Leadership in today's political arena is sometimes hard to see. So many times the buzzwords, self-promoters, and headlines are the only taste Oregonians get of what is going on in their state government.

Despite the critics and sound bytes, I believe ten percent of people serving in government seem to hold the other ninety percent together. I use the term "ten-percenters." These people never seek the headlines, or switch like a traffic light between what's politically expedient and what's right. They don't change their tune for self-interest lobby contributions, and don't compromise their core beliefs. Yet these ten-percenters are sought after to craft laws and sensible compromises. Their integrity and approach to service is based on what is best for other people, not their own egos.

It seems that this phenomenon is true in every state legislature in Oregon history, other state legislatures, and in every Congress I've studied. Politicians and grand-standers seem to get the headlines and are busy taking credit, but ten-percenters hold it together. Not Republican, and not Democrat. Just the best of the best of humble servants moving Oregon in the right direction.

Teaching a weekly informal history/public policy course to Senate floor staff and a few other Senate staffers, most of whom are between college and graduate school, I have tested the ten percent rule in the Oregon Senate, challenging every student to prove me right or wrong. But if, after observing the Oregon Senate in action for six months, they agree ten percent of Oregon Senators hold the other 90 percent together, then I asked them to write the Senators' names down on paper on our last day.

Each time I have done this the names the students write down are nearly all the same. Some Democrat. Some Republican. But never the grandstanders or the self-promot-ers. Somehow, the Senate floor staff know who is effective, who is not, who is humble, who works to make Oregon better, or who is only thinking about the next election.

Coming from all political persuasions and all corners of Oregon to get their first taste of public service, these student staffers are brilliant young people who quickly see what most Oregonians never will. They know the difference between bull and steak.

The real question is why only ten percent? Would Oregon be better if fifteen percent pursued service the same way? Would Oregon be better off we did not reward bad behavior and critics with headlines, but told the story of humble servants who work tirelessly on behalf of people?

Ten-percenters are not for sale. They make decisions based on what they view is right, regardless of the politics.

Ten-percenters make you feel important. They don't look over your shoulder while you're talking to them to see if someone more important just walked in the door.

Ten-percenters are thoughtful and wrestle with issues that they have never faced before, rather than relying upon the pat answer or quick party line.

After I decided to run for governor, I spoke about the difference in wanting to "be governor" verses "serving as governor."

I believe public service should not be an ego stroke, it is a commitment. It should not be a balancing act between polls, editorial boards, and lobbyists.

People who serve take body-blows. Winston Churchill once quipped, "in war you can die once, in politics you can die many times." Serving can be difficult, lonely work that requires "staying at the helm" tirelessly.

Oregonians need to know, there is a core of the finest people, publicly elected, who are making the sacrifice to serve. I know that if the light were shone on these people the ethic of public service would change. In fact, if the ten-percenters in public service were mined to become just fifteen-percenters, just like *Profiles in Courage*'s and JFK's Presidency had an effect on an American generation, Oregon would have a renewed appreciation and commitment. Not only to public service, but also to community service. If you knew the stories of Oregon's best, some of the people you have voted for, you would be inspired to be involved.

I grew up watching my Dad stand alone in business and in service. He took harsh criticism and watched friends abandon him, yet he stood on principle and never moved. He's the strongest leader and best example of leadership I know.

The leaders that are the ten-percenters in the legislature have also shown that same kind of integrity. I am determined to emulate them. I am determined to use political will and courage to do what's right for Oregonians. I find that determination on the campaign trail as I meet Oregonians behind the scenes, people who are working hard, dedicated to their families and who genuinely desire to believe in Oregon again.

POWER AT THE
KITCHEN TABLE

G et a load of this:

"If ordinary people don't understand what government is doing, then what government is doing probably isn't right. Government doesn't have to be complicated. Bureaucrats, politicians, and lobbyists defend its complexity in today's complex work because if government is kept out of the reach of ordinary citizen they can stay in charge. By self-definition, they become indispensable."

—FORMER WISCONSIN GOVERNOR AND REFORMER
TOMMY THOMPSON

It seems this phenomenon, where complexity is defended and government is out of reach, occurs about every 100 years. It happened early last century in Oregon and it is happening again. To best understand today, you must first see how a small group of citizens sitting around a kitchen table were able to overturn a political agenda which had run amok 100 years ago. In order to tell the story properly we need to go back to the creation of our state. Don't worry, this is a thrilling ride!

On Valentine's Day, 1859, Oregon became the 31st state in the Union and, using someone's copy of the laws of Iowa, we created a constitution, a part-time house of representatives, a state senate, an executive branch, and a judiciary in Salem.

At the time, the Federal Constitution dictated that the people could vote for a Federal Congressman, but the selection of U.S. Senators was left to the state legislature to decide.

The gamesmanship to become selected, or to stay in the U.S. Senate, took one giant leap away from people and one huge step towards self-interests. The railroad companies had "relationship builders." In modern language, they had lobbyists. Upstart state representatives and state senators needed to deliver for their communities and getting the railroad was one big incentive. The power of the railroads grew with each inch of track.

In those days, railroads were given alternating sections of land where their tracks touched. The West became a checkerboard of 640-acre sections, on the left and right, following each train. Over time, the railroads became the powerhouse for development.

For instance, my home town of Jacksonville, once the bustling center of Jackson county, the gold rush, and a cultural center, found itself in a dispute over to pay or not to pay the railroad for coming through its economically prosperous town. The railroad, I can imagine laughingly, refused to negotiate, and brought the line up through a small village a few miles away called Medfurd. Jacksonville nearly vanished overnight, (until the historical restoration movement found it again in the mid 1970's) and Medfurd became Medford.

The prize for the railroads was not decisions between a small town like Jacksonville or Medford, the power was in the control of the U.S. Senate and appropriations for further expansion. Therefore the real interest in Salem was to make sure friendly U.S. Senators stayed elected. And in order to continue the status quo, they needed to make sure "friendlies" stayed in power in Salem.

At the turn of the century, three major national shifts occurred that gave people the power to question if this cozy arrangement, special interests that demanded loyalty from politicians as a way to stay in power, was in their best interest.

First, President William McKinley was assassinated. A "trust buster" named Theodore Roosevelt became President.

Teddy Roosevelt, a New York blue-blood, had an independent, determined, fearless style and a mistrust of big business monopolies. Roosevelt, a reformer, frustrated the business plans of his social friends, J. P. Morgan, John D. Rockefeller, and Edward H. Harriman.

Second, Wisconsin's Republican Party gave birth to a national movement called "Progressivism." Progressives tied together individualism, traditional values, and concern for the needs of working people and the poor. Wisconsin's Progressive Robert "fighting Bob" La Follette, and his progressive colleges across the country believed the states were America's "laboratories of democracy." They believed the federal government was no longer responsive to ordinary citizens, that self-interests controlled the agenda to maintain the status quo.

America was just over one hundred years old, and the Progressives started a revolution to have government become responsive to people's needs again, not to the whims of a small group of elites. The movement gained supporters from both Democrats and Republicans.

As Governor of New Jersey and early Progressive, Woodrow Wilson stated, *"I suspect that the people of the United States understand their own interests better than any group of men in the confines of the country understand them. I don't want a smug lot of experts to sit down behind closed doors in Washington and play providence to me.*" President Theodore Roosevelt called Progressivism the *"highest and wisest form of conservatism.*"

The Wisconsin Progressives wanted people on level with their government, so they created the referendum, the primary, and the recall. They later became the first state in the nation to establish worker protections like unemployment insurance and workers' compensation.

The third big shift happened in Oregon. Oregon became Wisconsin's soul mate. In 1902 Oregon adopted the initiative system. The people were on level with their government. Government could address their needs or the people would govern themselves.

Just after the turn of the century self-interests controlled Oregon's state legislature and, in turn, who became Oregon's U.S. Senator. That was until a small group of frustrated citizens in Oregon City sat around a kitchen table and developed a people's campaign and initiative for direct election of U.S. Senators.

This is the heart of our story: with old-fashioned banners, terribly slow communications through mail, limited resources in the shadow of railroad wealth, and spreading national enthusiasm for returning power to people, Oregonians, through our initiative system, sparked a national debate leading to the 17th Constitutional Amendment[1] which created direct election of U.S. Senators. The national movement continued, with another push from grassroots Portland, for the ratification of 19th Amendment[2] giving women the right to vote.

One hundred years ago, Oregonians wanted their government back and they took it back.

Today the same revolutionary progressive ideas are bubbling below the surface ready to explode if given an opportunity to vent.

Unfortunately, the initiative system is completely under attack. Big business and big labor have joined forces to create hurdles and obstacles in the way of citizens who choose to use the system. Politicians in various offices who oppose our citizens' right to petition have written administrative rules, administrative procedures, and passed bills to make it more difficult, almost guaranteeing the process ends up in court.

Certainly there are abuses from ballot-title shopping; the increased pressure to get signatures at all cost, and the huge amount of money self-interests can pour into campaigns. Instead of fixing the problems, like taking the court out of choosing ballot titles and allowing signatures to be valid for two years, political leaders would rather scrap the entire system. They think Oregonians are not smart enough to know what they are voting for and that they know better what is good for Oregon.

What gave us direct election of U.S. Senators and women the right to vote is the accepted scapegoat for all of state government's problems one hundred years later. "If we just didn't have the threat of an initiative," I had heard so often in the Capitol, "we could get XYZ done." But isn't that the point? Without a check, the government can run roughshod over the people.

For example, over the last six years, the legislature has threatened people if they don't vote a tax increase. "Essential services will be cut." They say, "It's a threat— if they don't see it our way, we'll make it hurt." When the people rejected taxes, state police and education were cut. The people spoke clearly on issues ranging from land-use to marriage, taxes to forfeiture rights, and self-interests have worked time and time again to overturn, bog down in the courts, or find a creative way around, the will of the people.

Are the people frustrated? Yes. People want their government responsive; they want government to prioritize spending just like the people must do to make ends meet. They want the government to work at finding solutions, not at finding the next polarizing political issue that will keep one party in office.

I support the will of the voter and returning power to the people. The new generation of leaders in Oregon knows, just like the new generation of leaders one hundred years ago knew, they represent people, not just the elite.

As it was then, it is now: time for ordinary people to understand what government is doing. Government does not have to be complicated for complexity sake, but it does have to be credible, consistent, and respect people again.

A WORD ON PERS

Nearly one hundred years ago, the same time that Oregonians adopted legislative initiatives and workers compensation insurance, labor unions were gaining power to combat abuses. Unions were created to give workers better pay and more say with their employers. Unions protected wages, working conditions, and later retirements for union membership. Unfortunately, even with the noblest of intent, for the last twenty years, many self-interests in Oregon have gone too far at the expense of ordinary citizens.

Take the Public Employees Retirement System for example. Administrative rules (written by politicians and the self-interests that helped put them there) have been written to commit taxpayer monies to retiring workers through a defined benefit. Regardless of how the economy was doing (which governs how private citizens retirements are grown) the Public Employees Retirement System would continue payouts. Taxpayer debt obligation became higher than the cost of governing ourselves.

Am I against the Public Employee Retirement System? Absolutely not. But I am against abuse of power and the PERS system has nearly bankrupted our state.

The Governor appoints the people who make the decisions for PERS. Many of those appointed by the Governor have PERS accounts. Therefore they were making decisions that directly affected their own finances. This is called self-dealing, and it ought to be eliminated. Take the case of many of public company bankruptcies you seen on the TV news each night. Executives are going to jail because of self-dealing. They cooked the books, did not play by the rules everyone else must live by, got caught, and now their mega-business, their mega-homes and mega-wealth are going before bankruptcy judges. Because of self-dealing, millions of lives across the country are affected and billions of dollars will end up being repaid by either former investors or taxpayers. Self-dealing tempts those in the system to give themselves sweetheart deals.

For example, in 1980 if someone retired in Oregon's PERS system after 25 or 30 years of service to Oregon they would receive 50% of their final salary, including their earned social security, in retirement. In 1993, the rate moved to between 75% to 85%, plus their earned social security. By 2003, one out of four retirees were receiving more than 100% of their final salaries in retirements, not including their earned social security! Self-dealing helped to create this situation.

Oregonians were outraged when a major newspaper published a picture of two Oregon retirees recently retired and in their early fifties making more money sitting poolside in Arizona than working in Oregon. Who is paying for this? Taxpayers... you are paying for it. Moreover, our schools, our senior citizens, and our state troopers are not being funded at levels Oregonians demand, largely because of our obligation to pay PERS first.

In private business, directors of investor's trusts, who are running a large business or a bank, must, by law, carry insurance. If they make a bad decision, or are found to be self-dealing, they could be held personally liable and their insurance will protect the investor. This liability insurance is called "errors and omissions" insurance. PERS directors have no such policy.

PERS directors do have the authority to lower the rate they pay out to retirees to protect the entire PERS system. For instance, if the investments of PERS did not do so well on a given year, which happens, then they could temporarily lower the payout amount to protect future payouts and keep the system healthy. In 2000, 2001, 2002,

PERS bled money, losing huge amounts. But the board never lowered the rate to protect the plan for the long haul. Today, retirees have a less certain retirement plan and taxpayers have a whopping bill.

In 2003, the Oregon legislature tried to "fix" PERS by moving to a defined contribution instead of a defined benefit. This meant the state would contribute a set amount for retirees, but not guarantee a payout if PERS investments did not perform. Some reform was passed, but not enough. Oregonians were still outraged when people would retire, make more money than when they were working, and then be hired back. "Double-dipping" became the buzzword on everyone's lips. Double-dipping isn't fair.

Unfortunately, as with so many other examples, many hard working public employees are not aware that those making decisions for their retirement have not managed the system for the long-term.

Let me give some solutions that would be fair and would **protect** public employee retirees with responsible fiscal management:

1. The state of Oregon should pay for PERS board members to be covered by liability insurance for their potential "errors and omissions", and, if found to be self-dealing, decision-makers should be held personally responsible.

2. Eliminate double-dipping. I believe one job should only get one check. Some of our most valued public employees want to come back to work, and frankly, we need them. However, not by paying them twice through double-dipping. If employees want to come back to work, they can come back on contract or on agreement.

3. Taxpayers should not be left on the hook to pay a retirement that is higher than the retiree's previous salary.

4. Employees should be able to decide for themselves who manages their retirement money and how it's managed. PERS members should be able to opt out and take their money into a private account, much like a 401k account.

5. Create a true 401k plan with state contributions up to 6% and move anyone who could be in a position to "self-deal" into this plan. That would include the executive branch, state lawmakers, and even PERS board members. Get them out of the plan they manage.

7. Finally, put people on the board that would be selected to manage the system for the long haul. The PERS system is not healthy and Oregonians are on the tab to pay out for past mistakes. Our

schools, state troopers, and even our most vulnerable are paid second, third, and fourth behind this behemoth of debt and it must be stopped. Oregon made a promise to retirees, and Oregon will keep its word, but that is no reason to perpetuate the errors that were made in the past. PERS board members must lower the rates when investments drop and deficits grow, in order to protect PERS and taxpayers for the future.

Transparency in government must start in the secret world of PERS. Sweetheart deals are not fair.

Oregonians who have made a career in civil service deserve a retirement system that is fair, balanced, transparent and is managed for the long haul. Frankly, so do taxpayers.

MAKE YOUR MOM PROUD

I asked a kid who was my guest at the legislature, "Do you know why we do this?"

"To pass laws!"

Like many people he was taken up with the signs of power and wealth that surrounded us— and the prospect of being able to make people do things. Instinctively I shot back,

"No, we do this to make our Mom's proud."

I can't get away from the fact that the most important thing a politician can do is to build good character, stay true to their mandate, and not betray themselves, or their electorate, with shallow or misleading words. In my years in politics I quickly realized that in order to live happily with myself I would have to stay true to why I am in public life.

I do not believe in "selling out" for a vote, a contribution, or a quick headline. Therefore, even though critics in this campaign for governor protest, I still will not grandstand for press. It's hard, but often the "easy out" for an election is not being honest with who I am or why I am running. I have also seen, during my eight years, what happens to people who hold on to political power so tightly that they forget why it was given to them in the first place. It's easy to allow yourself to be defined by position or title and let politics go to your head, but I love to laugh, especially at myself.

I believe political position and authority are based on trust. You can't hang onto it with ego and threats.

But you know as well as I do that politics is particularly challenging to character building! This is why JFK said, "Mothers all want their sons to grow up to be president but they don't want them to become politicians in the process." There is just something about politics that either attracts people for the wrong reasons or makes people especially skeptical. I believe, however, that there is something that can lift us out of the malaise of politics: a character-driven approach which puts the issues in front of personalities.

As I've said earlier, as much as glamour and scepticism surround political power, I have been deeply moved by those who had true character and let the issues they stood for overshadow their own egos. In this book, I have tried to give you a clear sense of what needs to be turned around in this state for us to walk into a better future together.

Before you lay this book aside I want to give this one more shot because, ultimately, this book is not about me getting elected Governor—it is about the issues that we need to address the question we must ask ourselves: Do we want to go where we are headed.

Don't get me wrong: I want to be elected. But the reason I want to be elected is so that I can represent you on the issues that really count and allow you to believe in public service again and fix the direction of our state.

I invite you to ask yourself what you really want and to pick your candidate.

My bond with you is based on one word: respect. As your Governor I will wake up each day and work for that one Oregonian that does not have a job, that high school graduate who is thinking about leaving Oregon for more affordable college, that struggling family trying to move from renting into their first home, and the Susans of Oregon who just need a friend.

Specifically, within the first one hundred days of my administration I want to pass the K-thru-12 budget, lock up sexual predators by passing Jessica's law, and eliminate the Capital Gains Tax. I want to provide clear, credible and accountable spending of your money from the classrooms to social services. I will work with the legislature to regain your trust. Hopefully, I will restore your faith in Oregon.

I've tried to tell you about my approach so that you could get to know me. But more important than that are what we will stand for together. If we stand for these issues, I'm sure that our mothers could be proud of the politics in Oregon!

The reason I ask you to support me in this campaign, is that your support is truly what it is all about. What matters in the long run is not an election. What matters is that these solutions are put in place, that you have power returned to you, and Oregon is fixed. What I stand for can only happen if we pledge ourselves together to making it happen. I want to work with you because you matter.

The way to create a better Oregon is to not delegate it to anyone else.

1 (Passed by Congress May 13, 1912. Ratified April 8, 1913)
2 (Passed by Congress June 4, 1919. Ratified August 18, 1920.)